21st Century Folk Hymnal

Melody/guitar edition

Compiled and edited by
Kevin Mayhew

CW01335730

Kevin
Mayhew

We hope you enjoy the music in this book. Further copies are available
from your local music shop or Christian bookshop.

In case of difficulty, please contact the publisher direct:

The Sales Department
KEVIN MAYHEW LTD
Buxhall
Stowmarket
Suffolk
IP14 3DJ

Phone 01449 737978
Fax 01449 737834
E-mail info@kevinmayhewltd.com

Please ask for our complete catalogue of outstanding Church Music.

21st Century Folk Hymnal is available as follows:

1413094 Keyboard/Instrumental edition.

1413091 Melody/Guitar edition.

1480055 A boxed collection of five CDs containing all 100 songs.

1490039 A boxed collection of five cassettes containing all 100 songs.

With the exception of those settings by Jacques Berthier and Margaret Rizza all
the keyboard and instrumental arrangements in the book are by Keith Stent.

First published in Great Britain in 1999 by Kevin Mayhew Ltd.

ISBN 1 84003 313 4
ISMN M 57004 508 2
Catalogue No: 1413091

0 1 2 3 4 5 6 7 8 9

Cover illustration and design by Jonathan Stroulger
Music setting by Chris Hinkins
Proof-reader: Helen Goodall
Project co-ordinator: Janet Simpson

Printed and bound in Great Britain

Important Copyright Information

The Publishers wish to express their gratitude to the copyright owners who have granted permission to include their copyright material in this book. Full details are clearly indicated on the respective pages.

The words of most of the songs in this publication are covered by a Church Copyright Licence which allows local church reproduction on overhead projector acetates, in service bulletins, songsheets, audio-visual recordings and other formats.

The music in this book is covered by the newly introduced 'add-on' Music Reproduction Licence issued by CCL (Europe) Ltd and you may photocopy the music and words of the songs in this book provided:

- You hold a current Music Reproduction Licence from CCL (Europe) Ltd.

- The copyright owner of the hymn or song you intend to photocopy is included in the Authorised Catalogue List which comes with your Music Reproduction Licence.

Full details of both the Christian Copyright Licence and the additional Music Reproduction Licence are available from:

Christian Copyright Licensing (Europe) Ltd
PO Box 1339
Eastbourne
East Sussex
BN21 4YF

Telephone: 01323 417711
Fax: 01323 417722

Please note, all the texts and music in this book are protected by copyright and if you do not possess a licence from CCL (Europe) Ltd, they may not be reproduced in any way for sale or private use without the consent of the copyright owner.

Every effort has been made to trace the owners of copyright material, and we hope that no copyright has been infringed. Pardon is sought and apology made if the contrary be the case, and a correction will be made in any reprint of this book.

1 Adoramus te, Domine Deus

Slow and calm

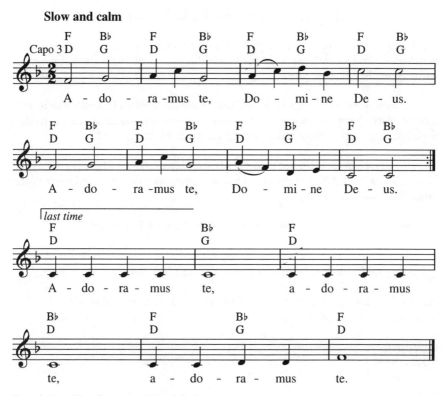

Translation: We adore you, O Lord God.

Words: Traditional
Music: Margaret Rizza

2 Alleluia! Magnificat!

A good way to sing this is as follows:

The 'Alleluia' is sung by a cantor then echoed by the congregation; the congregation continue to sing the 'Alleluia' while the cantor sings the verse; all then sing the 'Alleluia' together with instruments playing the instrumental descant (see accompaniment edition for parts).

Text and music: Communaté du Chemin Neuf, trans. Robert Kelly

Original text and music © Copyright ARTEMAS-CCN, 10 rue Henri IV, 69287 Lyon Cedex 02, France. Used by permission. Translation © Copyright 1999 Kevin Mayhew Ltd.

3 All heaven declares

1. All heav'n de-clares the glo-ry of the ri-sen Lord. Who can com-pare with the beau-ty of the Lord? For-e-ver he will be the Lamb up-on the throne. I glad-ly bow the knee and wor-ship him a-lone.

2. I will proclaim
   the glory of the risen Lord.
   Who once was slain
   to reconcile us all to God.
   For ever you will be
   the Lamb upon the throne.
   I gladly bow the knee
   and worship you alone.

Words and Music: Noel and Tricia Richards

4 All I once held dear *(Knowing you)*

Smoothly

1. All I once held dear, built my life up - on, all this world re-veres, and wars to own, all I once thought gain I have count-ed loss; spent and worth-less now, com - pared to this. Know-ing you, Je - sus, know-ing you, there is no great-er thing. You're my all, you're the best, you're my joy, my right-eous-ness, and I

1, 2. love you, Lord.

D.C. **3.** love you, Lord.

2. Now my heart's desire
   is to know you more,
   to be found in you
   and known as yours.
   To possess by faith
   what I could not earn,
   all-surpassing gift
   of righteousness.

3. Oh, to know the pow'r
   of your risen life,
   and to know you in
   your sufferings.
   To become like you
   in your death, my Lord,
   so with you to live
   and never die.

Words, based on Philippians 3: 8-12, and Music: Graham Kendrick

5 All through the years

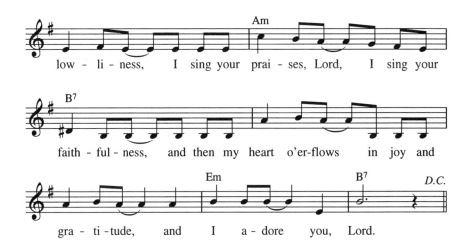

low - li - ness, I sing your prai - ses, Lord, I sing your

faith - ful - ness, and then my heart o'er-flows in joy and

gra - ti -tude, and I a - dore you, Lord.

2. Your grace has overflowed, your love enfolded me,
   and all my weaknesses have been a strength to me;
   and then my heart o'erflows in joy and gratitude,
   and I adore you, Lord.

3. Show me the way, O Lord, to be more firm and true,
   to spend the years to come in greater love of you,
   and let my heart o'erflow in joy and gratitude,
   and I'll adore you, Lord.

Words and Music: Marie Lydia Pereira

6 Arise, Zion

Firmly

Refrain

A - rise, Zi - on, a - rise, for your light has come, your
light has come! A - rise, Zi - on, a - rise, for the
Light of the World has come! 1. See how the dark-ness sur-
rounds you and night still co-vers the earth; but now, look
up at the ra-diance a - bout you, dawn-ing with the Sa-viour's birth.

2. Hear how the nations are weeping,
   and violence sweeps through the world.
   Take heart!
   For here is the peace you are seeking;
   God himself will be with you.

3. Hear how our people are crying:
   they search for reasons to live.
   Behold!
   In Bethlehem town lies the answer:
   God now sends your Shepherd true.

Words and Music: Francesca Leftley

7 As the deer pants for the water

Flowing

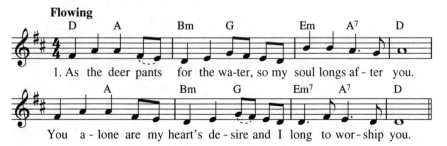

1. As the deer pants for the wa-ter, so my soul longs af - ter you.
You a - lone are my heart's de - sire and I long to wor-ship you.

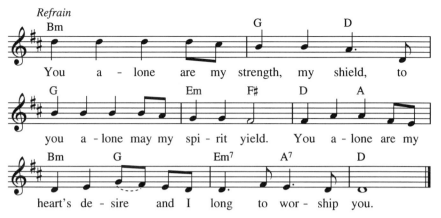

Refrain

You a-lone are my strength, my shield, to you a-lone may my spi-rit yield. You a-lone are my heart's de-sire and I long to wor-ship you.

2. I want you more than gold or silver,
only you can satisfy.
You alone are the real joy-giver
and the apple of my eye.

3. You're my friend and you are my brother,
even though you are a King.
I love you more than any other,
so much more than anything.

Words and Music: Martin J. Nystrom

8 As we are gathered

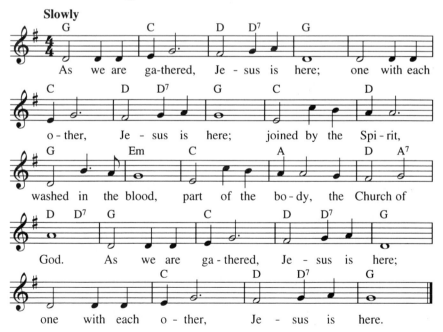

Slowly

As we are ga-thered, Je-sus is here; one with each o-ther, Je-sus is here; joined by the Spi-rit, washed in the blood, part of the bo-dy, the Church of God. As we are ga-thered, Je-sus is here; one with each o-ther, Je-sus is here.

Words and Music: John Daniels

9 Beauty for brokenness *(God of the poor)*

1. Beau-ty for bro-ken-ness, hope for des - pair, Lord, in the suff'- ring this is our prayer. Bread for the child - ren, jus-tice, joy, peace, sun-rise to sun - set your king-dom in - crease.

Refrain

God of the poor, friend of the weak, give us com - pas-sion, we pray, melt our cold hearts, let tears fall like rain. Come, change our love from a spark to a flame.

2. Shelter for fragile lives,
   cures for their ills,
   work for the craftsmen,
   trade for their skills.
   Land for the dispossessed,
   rights for the weak,
   voices to plead the cause
   of those who can't speak.

3. Refuge from cruel wars,
   havens from fear,
   cities for sanctu'ry,
   freedoms to share.
   Peace to the killing fields,
   scorched earth to green,
   Christ for the bitterness,
   his cross for the pain.

4. Rest for the ravaged earth,
   oceans and streams,
   plundered and poisoned,
   our future, our dreams.
   Lord, end our madness,
   carelessness, greed;
   make us content with
   the things that we need.

5. Lighten our darkness,
   breathe on this flame,
   until your justice
   burns brightly again;
   until the nations
   learn of your ways,
   seek your salvation
   and bring you their praise.

Words and Music: Graham Kendrick

10 Be still, for the presence of the Lord

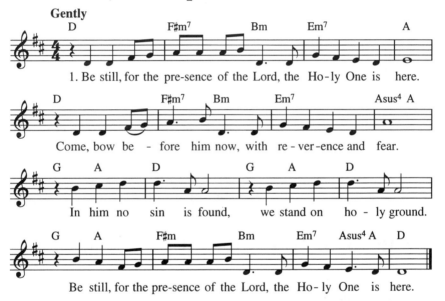

Gently

1. Be still, for the pre-sence of the Lord, the Ho-ly One is here.

Come, bow be - fore him now, with re - ver-ence and fear.

In him no sin is found, we stand on ho - ly ground.

Be still, for the pre-sence of the Lord, the Ho-ly One is here.

2. Be still, for the glory of the Lord is shining all around;
   he burns with holy fire, with splendour he is crowned.
   How awesome is the sight, our radiant King of light!
   Be still, for the glory of the Lord is shining all around.

3. Be still, for the power of the Lord is moving in this place;
   he comes to cleanse and heal, to minister his grace.
   No work too hard for him, in faith receive from him.
   Be still, for the power of the Lord is moving in this place.

Words and Music: David J. Evans

11 Blessed be God

Broadly

Refrain

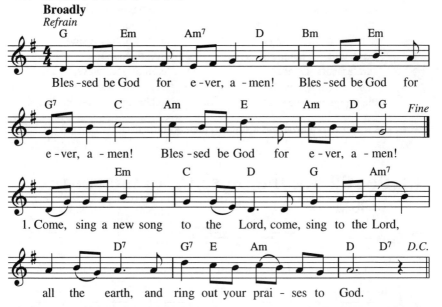

Bles-sed be God for e-ver, a-men! Bles-sed be God for
e-ver, a-men! Bles-sed be God for e-ver, a-men!

1. Come, sing a new song to the Lord, come, sing to the Lord,
all the earth, and ring out your prai-ses to God.

2. Come, tell of all his wondrous deeds,
   come, thank him for all he has done,
   and offer your gifts to the Lord.

3. Let all creation shout for joy,
   come, worship the Lord in his house,
   the Lord who made heaven and earth.

Words, based on Psalm 95: Hubert J. Richards
Music: Richard Lloyd
© Copyright 1999 Kevin Mayhew Ltd.

12 Bless the Lord, my soul

Bouncy

Refrain

Bless the Lord, my soul! Bless the Lord, my soul! Let
all that is with-in me praise his name!
Bless the Lord, my soul! Bless the Lord, my soul! Let

© Copyright 1999 Kevin Mayhew Ltd.

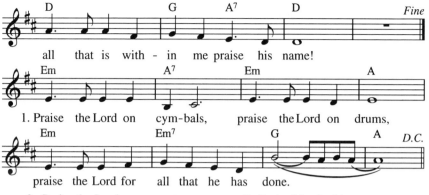

all that is with-in me praise his name!

1. Praise the Lord on cym-bals, praise the Lord on drums,

praise the Lord for all that he has done.

2. Praise the Lord on trumpet,
   praise the Lord in song,
   praise him all who stand
   before his throne.

3. Praise him for his mercy,
   praise him for his pow'r,
   praise him for his love
   which conquers all.

Words and Music: Mike Anderson

13 Blest are you, Lord

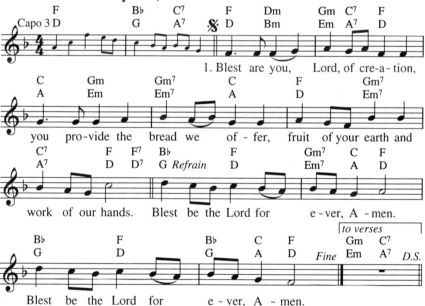

1. Blest are you, Lord, of cre-a-tion,

you pro-vide the bread we of-fer, fruit of your earth and

work of our hands. Blest be the Lord for e-ver, A-men.

Blest be the Lord for e-ver, A-men.

2. Blest are you, Lord of creation,
   you provide the wine we offer,
   fruit of your earth and work of our hands.

3. Blest are you, Lord of creation,
   look with favour on our off'rings,
   pour out your Spirit over these gifts.

Words: based on the Offertory prayers: Hubert J. Richards
Music: Richard Shephard

14 Calm me, Lord

Tranquil

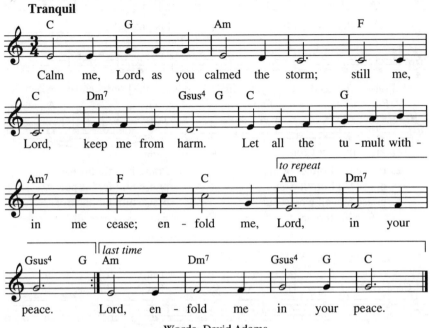

Calm me, Lord, as you calmed the storm; still me,
Lord, keep me from harm. Let all the tu -mult with -
in me cease; en - fold me, Lord, in your
peace. Lord, en - fold me in your peace.

Words: David Adams
Music: Margaret Rizza

15 Change my heart, O God

With feeling

Change my heart, O God, make it e -ver true;
Change my heart, O God, may I be like

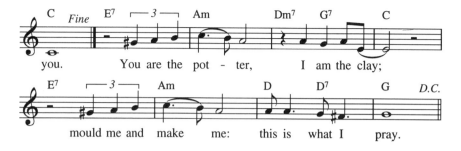

you. You are the pot - ter, I am the clay;

mould me and make me: this is what I pray.

Words, based on Isaiah 64:8, and Music: Eddie Espinosa

16 Come, Holy Spirit

1. Come, Ho - ly Spi - rit, give us new life from a - bove;

come, Ho - ly Spi - rit, with your high-est gift of love.

Refrain

Faith, hope and love, these three en - dure for e - ver.

Faith, hope and love, the great-est of these is love.

2. True, kind and patient,
   love will keep no score of wrongs;
   come, Holy Spirit,
   let our spirits join your song.

3. Wisdom is passing,
   knowledge vanishes away;
   come, Holy Spirit,
   lead us in your perfect way.

Words: Michael Forster
Music: Kevin Mayhew
© Copyright 1999 Kevin Mayhew Ltd.

17 Come, O Lord, inspire us

Refrain

Come, O Lord, in-spire us with the pow'r of your love, that your
Word may take flesh, that your king-dom may come.
Come, O Lord, in-spire us with the pow'r of your love, that your
Name may be sung and your will may be done.

1. When the poor are lif - ted up, and when the weak are strong,
we have the right to sing 'Al - le - lu - ia!'
When the migh-ty are laid low, the dis-pos-sessed made rich,
we have the right to sing 'Al - le - lu - ia!'

2. When the hungry want no more
   and when the sick are healed,
   we have the right to sing 'Alleluia!'
   When the darkness holds no fear
   and each new dawn brings hope,
   we have the right to sing 'Alleluia!'

3. When the pow'r of hate lies crushed
   and there's no ground for war,
   we have the right to sing 'Alleluia!'
   When the lion and the lamb
   lie peaceful, all is calm,
   we have the right to sing 'Alleluia!'

Words and Music: Frances M. Kelly
© Copyright 1999 Kevin Mayhew Ltd.

18 Come on and celebrate!

Words and Music: Patricia Morgan and Dave Bankhead

19 Come to me

Gently

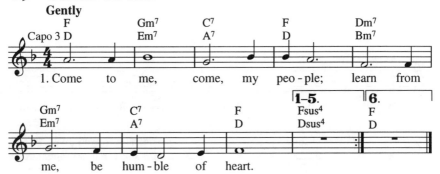

1. Come to me, come, my peo-ple; learn from
   me, be hum-ble of heart.

2. I your Lord, I your master;
   learn from me, be humble of heart.

3. Follow me to my Father;
   learn from me, be humble of heart.

4. In my death, in my rising;
   learn from me, be humble of heart.

5. Be transformed by my Spirit;
   learn from me, be humble of heart.

6. Glory be to my Father;
   learn from me, be humble of heart.

Words and Music: Gerard Markland

20 Dance in your Spirit

Brightly

Dance in your Spi-rit, we dance in your Spi-rit, we
dance in your Spi-rit of joy!
joy! 1. Je-sus, you showed us the way to
live, and your Spi-rit sets us free,

free now to sing, free to dance and shout, 'Glo - ry, glo ry' to your name.

2. Jesus, you opened your arms for us,
but we nailed them to the cross;
but you are risen and now we live,
free from, free from ev'ry fear.

3. Your Spirit brings peace and gentleness,
kindness, self-control and love,
patience and goodness and faith and joy,
Spirit, Spirit fill us now.

21 Deep within my heart

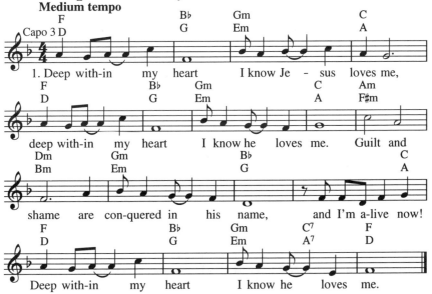

1. Deep with-in my heart I know Je - sus loves me,
deep with-in my heart I know he loves me. Guilt and
shame are con-quered in his name, and I'm a-live now!
Deep with-in my heart I know he loves me.

2. Deep within my heart I know I'm forgiven,
deep within my heart I know that I'm free.
Free from sin, a new life to begin, and I'm alive now.
Deep within my heart I know that I'm free.

3. Deep within my heart Jesus' love is healing,
deep within my heart he is healing me.
Tears like rain are flooding out the pain, and I'm alive now.
Deep within my heart he is healing me.

22 Don't build your house

Don't build your house on the san - dy land,
don't build it too near the shore. Well, it
might look kind of nice, but you'll have to build it twice, oh, you'll
have to build your house once more. You'd bet - ter
build your house up - on a rock, make a
good foun - da - tion on a sol - id spot. oh, the storms may
come and go but the peace of God you will know.

This song can be sung as a round with the second voices entering at **B**

Words and Music: Karen Lafferty

23 Exaudi nos, Domine

Ex - au - di nos, Do - mi - ne;

do - na no - bis pa - cem tu - am.

Translation: Hear us, O Lord, give us your peace.

Words: Traditional

Music: Margaret Rizza

24 Father God, gentle Father God

Gently

Fa - ther God, gen - tle Fa - ther God,
my Lord of con - so - la - tion,
I lift up my heart to you.

1. O Lord, you search me, you know me, my ev - 'ry move.

My thoughts you read from a - far, all my ways lie there be - fore you.

2. My heart, my innermost being
   was made by you.
   My body, secretly formed in the womb,
   was always with you.

3. What place, what heavens could
   hide me away from you?
   Were I to fly to the ends of the sea,
   your hand would guide me.

4. Your works, your knowledge, your love
   are beyond my mind.
   My Lord, I thank you for these
   and the wonder of my being.

5. O Lord, come search me, come find
   what is in my heart;
   that I may never stray far
   from your path of life eternal.

Words, based on Psalm 138 (139), and Music: Gerard Markland

25 Father God, we worship you

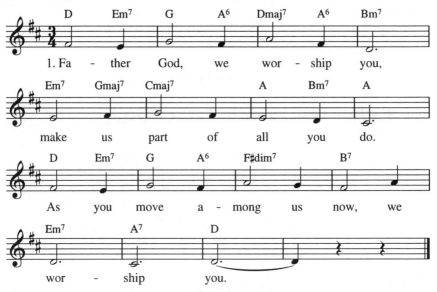

1. Fa - ther God, we wor - ship you,
make us part of all you do.
As you move a - mong us now, we
wor - ship you.

2. Jesus King, we worship you,
   help us listen now to you.
   As you move among us now
   we worship you.

3. Spirit pure, we worship you,
   with your fire our zeal renew.
   As you move among us now
   we worship you.

Words and Music: Graham Kendrick

26 From heaven you came *(The Servant King)*

1. From heav'n you came, help - less babe,

2. There in the garden of tears,
my heavy load he chose to bear;
his heart with sorrow was torn.
'Yet not my will but yours,' he said.

3. Come see his hands and his feet,
the scars that speak of sacrifice,
hands that flung stars into space,
to cruel nails surrendered.

4. So let us learn how to serve,
and in our lives enthrone him;
each other's needs to prefer,
for it is Christ we're serving.

Words and Music: Graham Kendrick

27 From the sun's rising

Steadily

1. From the sun's ris-ing un-to the sun's set-ting,
Je-sus, our Lord, shall be great in the earth;
and all earth's king-doms shall be his do-min-ion,
all of cre-a-tion shall sing of his worth.

Refrain
Let ev-'ry heart, ev-'ry voice, ev-'ry tongue join with
spi - rits a - blaze; one in his love, we will
cir-cle the world with the song of his praise. O,
let all his peo-ple re - joice, and
let all the earth hear his voice.

2. To ev'ry tongue, tribe and nation he sends us,
to make disciples to teach and baptise.
For all authority to him is given;
now, as his witnesses, we shall arise.

3. Come, let us join with the church from all nations,
cross ev'ry border, throw wide ev'ry door;
workers with him as he gathers his harvest,
till earth's far corners our Saviour adore.

Words and Music: Graham Kendrick

28 Give thanks with a grateful heart

Words and Music: Henry Smith

29 God cares for all creation

Medium tempo

1. God cares for all cre - a - tion as a shep-herd for the
sheep he is ev - 'ry-thing the world can e - ver need.
In green and peace-ful pla - ces, and where gen - tle wa-ters
flow, we'll fol-low him wher - e - ver he may lead.

Refrain
'I'm the shep - herd who cares for the sheep', he
says, 'and my pro-mise you know I will keep', he
says, 'though the path may be ro - cky and steep', he
says, 'I will love you and lead you for e - ver'.

2. Yes, even in the darkness,
   there's no need to be afraid
   in the shadow and
   the mystery of death;
   for God is always with us,
   giving confidence and hope,
   his spirit calms the trembling
   of our breath.

3. Though others may assail us,
   he assures us of his love,
   and prepares a feast
   so everyone will know.
   He comforts us with kindness,
   like a sweetly scented oil,
   while gladness and contentment
   overflow.

4. We know his love and goodness
   will be with us al our days,
   as we go in faith where he has gone before.
   His love will never falter,
   nor his ancient promise fail,
   and we shall live with him for evermore.

Words, based on Psalm 22 (23): Michael Forster
Music: Christopher Tambling

30 God is love

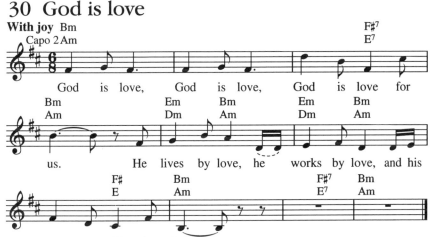

God is love, God is love, God is love for us.
He lives by love, he works by love, and his sun comes shi-ning through.

2. God is life, God is life,
   God is life for us.
   His life keeps us from sin and strife,
   and his sun comes shining through.

3. God is food, God is food,
   God is food for us.
   He is our food, our saving good,
   and his sun comes shining through.

4. God is light, God is light,
   God is light for us.
   His light shines out through the darkest night,
   and his sun comes shining through.

5. God is peace, God is peace.
   God is peace for us.
   And through his peace all quarrels cease,
   and his sun comes shining through.

6. God is joy, God is joy,
   God is joy for us.
   The purest joy, the deepest joy,
   and his sun comes shining through.

7. God is strength, God is strength,
   God is strength for us.
   The greatest strength, unfailing strength,
   and his sun comes shining through.

8. God is truth, God is truth,
   God is truth for us.
   The surest truth, unchanging truth,
   and his sun comes shining through.

Words and Music: Marie Lydia Pereira

31 Healer of the sick

1. Healer of the sick, Lord Jesus, Son of God,
Lord, how we long for you: walk here among us.

Refrain

Bind up our broken lives, comfort our broken hearts,
banish our hidden fears. Lord, come with pow'r,
bring new light to the blind, bring peace to troubled minds,
hold us now in your arms, set us free now.

2. Bearer of our pain,
   Lord Jesus, Lamb of God;
   Lord, how we cry to you:
   walk here among us.

3. Calmer of our fears,
   Lord Jesus, Prince of Peace;
   Lord, how we yearn for you:
   walk here among us.

4. Saviour of the world,
   Lord Jesus, mighty God;
   Lord, how we sing to you:
   walk here among us.

Words and Music: Francesca Leftley
© Copyright 1999 Kevin Mayhew Ltd.

32 Here is bread

2. Here is grace, here is peace,
   Christ is with us, he is with us;
   know his grace, find his peace,
   feast on Jesus here.

3. Here we are, joined in one,
   Christ is with us, he is with us;
   we'll proclaim, till he comes,
   Jesus crucified.

Words and Music: Graham Kendrick

33 How many years have I left here?
(My going-home day)

With movement

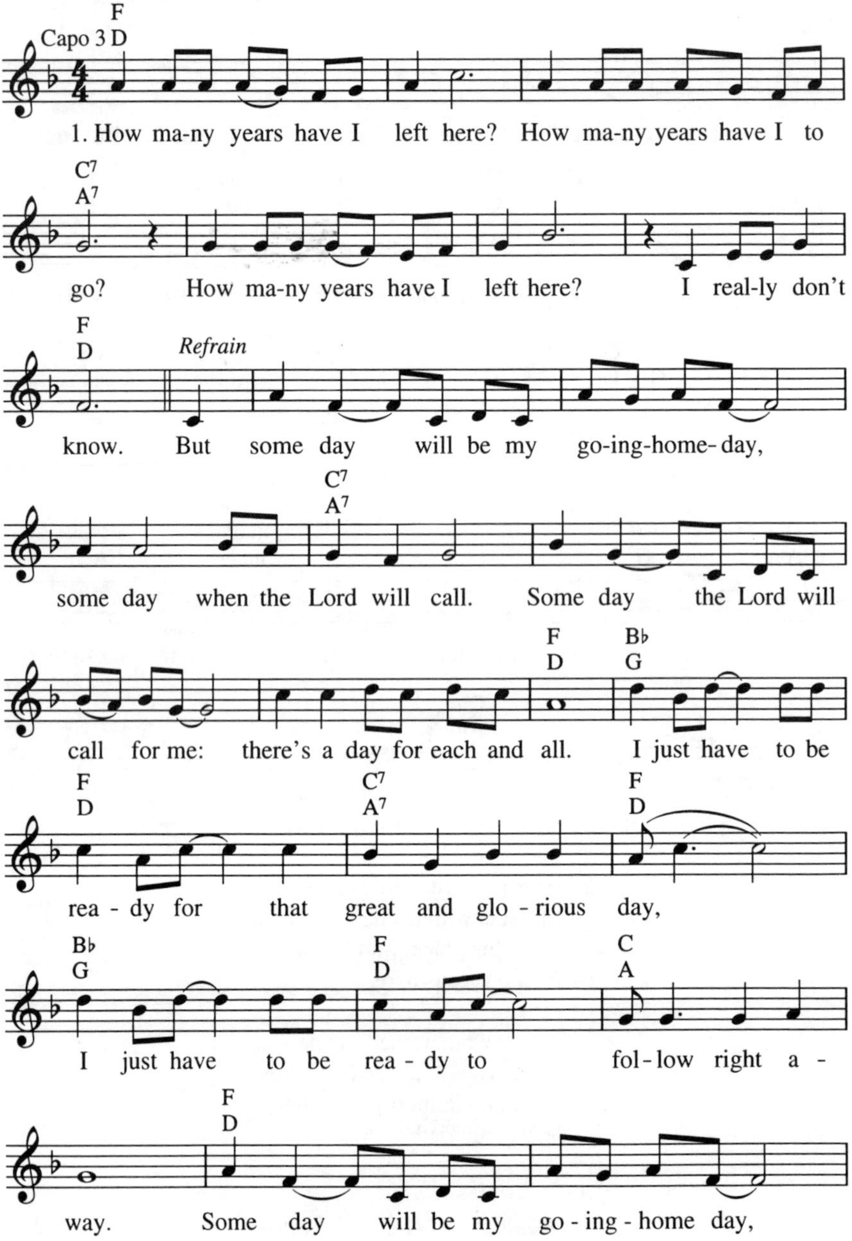

F
Capo 3 D
1. How ma-ny years have I left here? How ma-ny years have I to
C7
A7
go? How ma-ny years have I left here? I real-ly don't
F
D
Refrain
know. But some day will be my go-ing-home-day,
C7
A7
some day when the Lord will call. Some day the Lord will
F
D
B♭
G
call for me: there's a day for each and all. I just have to be
F
D
C7
A7
F
D
rea - dy for that great and glo - rious day,
B♭
G
F
D
C
A
I just have to be rea - dy to fol-low right a -
F
D
way. Some day will be my go - ing - home day,

some day when the Lord will call. Some day the Lord will

call for me: O Lord, keep me rea-dy for that call.

2. Will I be called in the morning
   or when the sun is setting low?
   Will I be called in the night time?
   I really don't know.

3. Will there be time for a farewell,
   will there be time to say adieu?
   Will there be time to say, 'sorry?'
   I really don't know.

Words and Music: Marie Lydia Pereira

34 I am the Good Shepherd

Gently with movement

Refrain

I am the Good Shep-herd and I know my

sheep, and they know me; and I lay down my

life for my sheep. 1. I am no hire-ling, I'll

not a-ban-don my sheep. Though the wolves ap-proach

I guard you still, my flock, your shep-herd.

2. But there are others who do not listen to me.
   I will bring them in, then there will be
   one flock, one shepherd.

3. The Father loves me because I lay down my life,
   given willingly so there will be
   one flock, one shepherd.

35 I look to the mountains

2. Lord of love, Lord who knows my name,
   slow to anger, rich in mercy,
   knows our faults, yet removes our sin,
   strong his love to those who fear him.

Words, based on Psalms 120 (121) and 102 (103), and Music: Gerard Markland

36 I need you, Lord

1. I need you, Lord. I need you, Lord.
I need you, Lord. I need you, Lord.
I need you, Lord. I need you, Lord.
I need you, Lord. I need you, Lord.

2. I need your love . . .

3. You died for me . . .

4. Forgive me, Lord . . .

5. You died but rose . . .

6. Your Spirit lives . . .

7. Come, live in me . . .

8. I need you, Lord . . .

Other phrases may be improvised to suit the occasion.

Words and Music: Mike Anderson
© Copyright 1999 Kevin Mayhew Ltd.

37 In the Lord is my joy

Andante

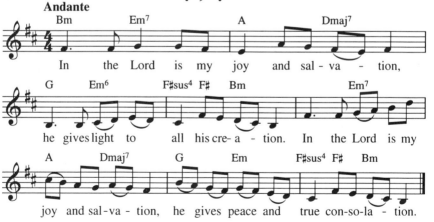

In the Lord is my joy and sal-va - tion, he gives light to all his cre-a - tion. In the Lord is my joy and sal-va - tion, he gives peace and true con-so-la - tion.

Words and Music: Margaret Rizza
© Copyright 1998 Kevin Mayhew Ltd.

38 Jesus is risen *(Resurrection song)*

With joy

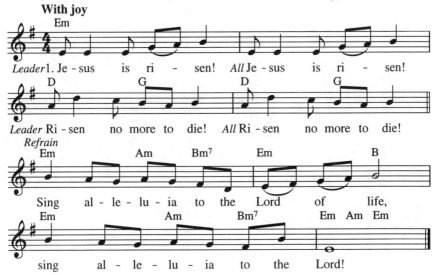

Leader 1. Je - sus is ri - sen! *All* Je - sus is ri - sen!

Leader Ri - sen no more to die! *All* Ri - sen no more to die!

Refrain

Sing al - le - lu - ia to the Lord of life,

sing al - le - lu - ia to the Lord!

2. Christ is the first-born!
   Christ is the first-born!
   We follow where he leads!
   We follow where he leads!

3. We are Christ's body!
   We are Christ's body!
   He is the cornerstone!
   He is the cornerstone!

Words and Music: Frances M. Kelly

39 Let love be real

With expression

Capo 3

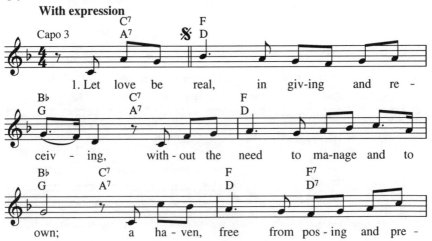

1. Let love be real, in giv-ing and re -

ceiv - ing, with - out the need to ma-nage and to

own; a ha - ven, free from pos - ing and pre -

tend - ing, where ev'ry weak - ness may be safe-ly
known. Give me your hand a - long the de - sert
path - way, give me your love wher - e - ver we may
go. As God loves us, so let us love each
o - ther: with no de-mands, just o - pen hands and space to

1, 2.
grow.   2. Let love be

3.
grow.

2. Let love be real, not grasping or confining,
   that strange embrace that holds yet sets us free;
   that helps us face the risk of truly living,
   and makes us brave to be what we might be.
   Give me your strength when all my words are weakness;
   give me your love in spite of all you know.

3. Let love be real, with no manipulation,
   no secret wish to harness or control;
   let us accept each other's incompleteness,
   and share the joy of learning to be whole.
   Give me your hope through dreams and disappointments;
   give me your trust when all my failings show.

Words: Michael Forster
Music: Christopher Tambling

40 Let our praise to you be as incense

Words, based on Psalm 140 (141) and Isaiah 6: Bryan Spinks
Music: Malcolm Archer

41 Let the heavens declare

Lively
Refrain

Let the hea-vens de-clare, let the moun-tains sing,
let the o-ceans roar that Je-sus lives and is our King.
Lift your hands in praise, let your spi-rits soar,
let the hea-vens de-clare, let the moun-tains sing, let the o-ceans
roar. 1. All the sins we've e-ver sinned died u-pon the
cross with him, but we know he lives a-gain:
the vic-t'ry is won, the vic-t'ry is won,
the vic-t'ry is won, the vic-t'ry is won.

2. Hanging on the cross for me
Jesus died in agony.
Blood and tears he shed for me,
that I might have life. (4)

3. In the kingdom he revealed
broken hearts can all be healed,
through the covenant he sealed
with his holy blood. (4)

Words and Music: Mike Anderson

42 Let us sing your glory

Steadily

1. Let us sing your glo-ry, Lord, al-le-lu - ia,
let us praise your name a - dored, al-le-lu - ia.
Joy and beau-ty come from you, al - le-lu - ia,
and each hour your love shines through, al - le-lu - ia.

Refrain
Al-le-lu - ia, al-le lu - ia, al-le-lu, al-le-lu - ia.

2. Leaf that quivers on the tree, alleluia,
flowers we delight to see, alleluia.
Planets as they reel in space, alleluia,
tell us of your power and grace, alleluia.

3. All creation sings your praise, alleluia,
young and old their voices raise, alleluia.
Children as they laugh and sing, alleluia,
to your goodness homage bring, alleluia.

Words and Music: Marie Lydia Pereira

43 Let us turn to Jesus

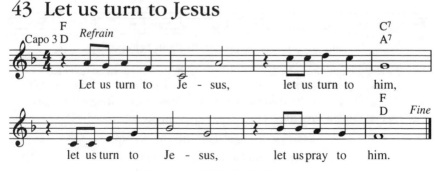

Refrain

Let us turn to Je - sus, let us turn to him,
let us turn to Je - sus, let us pray to him.

Fine

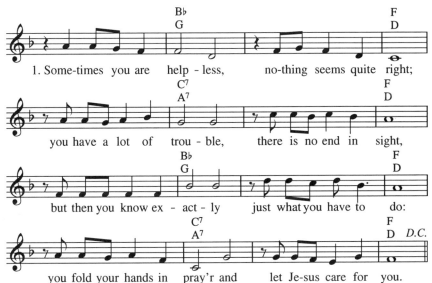

1. Some-times you are help-less, no-thing seems quite right;
you have a lot of trou-ble, there is no end in sight,
but then you know ex-act-ly just what you have to do:
you fold your hands in pray'r and let Je-sus care for you.

2. Sometimes you are crying,
   you've a broken heart;
   you have so many sorrows,
   you don't know where to start!

But then there comes, like sunshine,
a ray into your heart:
you fold your hands in pray'r,
let Jesus do his part.

Words and Music: Marie Lydia Pereira

44 Lift up the light of your face

Simply

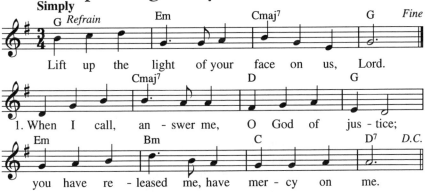

Lift up the light of your face on us, Lord.

1. When I call, an-swer me, O God of jus-tice;
you have re-leased me, have mer-cy on me.

2. God grants his favours to all his belovéd,
   he always hears me whenever I call.

3. So many asking, 'How can we be happy?'
   Lift up the light of your face on us, Lord!

4. I will lie down to rest, peacefully sleeping,
   knowing that you alone keep me secure.

Words, based on Psalm 4, and Music: Francesca Leftley

45 Lift up your heads

2. Up from the dead he ascends,
   through ev'ry rank of heav'nly pow'r.
   Let heav'n prepare the highest place,
   throw wide the everlasting doors.

3. With trumpet blast and shouts of joy,
   all heaven greets the risen King.
   With angel choirs come line the way,
   throw wide the gates and welcome him.

Words and Music: Graham Kendrick

46 Listen to me, Yahweh

2. Lord, in your goodness, please forgive me;
   listen to me, hear my plea.

3. Lord, you are merciful and faithful;
   turn to me now in my need.

4. Lord, give me strength, I am your servant;
   show me that you really care.

Words, based on Psalm 86, and Music: Mike Anderson

47 Listen to my voice
(A healing song)

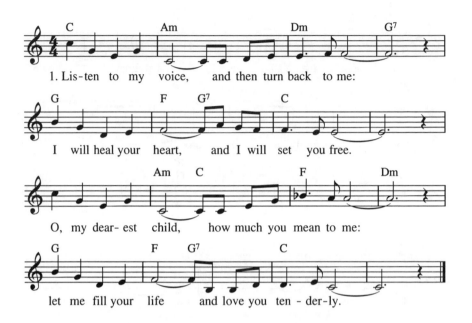

1. Lis-ten to my voice, and then turn back to me:
I will heal your heart, and I will set you free.
O, my dear-est child, how much you mean to me:
let me fill your life and love you ten-der-ly.

2. Rest within my arms and let your fears depart,
feel my peace and joy bind up your broken heart.
I will wipe your tears and make you whole again:
come to me, my child, and turn away from sin.

3. Take my hand, and now we will begin once more,
I will walk beside you as I did before.
I have never left you, though your eyes were dim:
walk with me in light, and turn away from sin.

Words and Music: Francesca Leftley
© Copyright 1999 Kevin Mayhew Ltd.

48 Lord of life

Majestically

Refrain

Lord of life, Lord of love, come, fill me with your love. Lord of life, Lord of love, come, live now in my heart.

1. You are clothed in ma-jes-ty, you set the waves u-pon the sea, come, wash me a-new with your love.

2. You are wrapped in radiant light,
   you are the Lord of day and night,
   come, lighten my life with your love.

3. All my sins you will forgive,
   for you alone I want to live,
   come, take me and fill me again.

Words and Music: Mike Anderson
© Copyright 1999 Kevin Mayhew Ltd.

49 Lord, the light of your love
(Shine, Jesus, shine)

Majestic and steady

1. Lord, the light of your
love is shin - ing, in the midst of the dark - ness, shin - ing;
Je - sus, Light of the World, shine up-on us, set us free by the
truth you now bring us. Shine on me, shine on me.

Refrain

Shine, Je -sus, shine, fill this land with the Fa-ther's glo - ry;
Flow, ri - ver, flow, flood the na - tions with grace and mer-cy;

1.
blaze, Spi - rit, blaze, set our hearts on fire.
send forth your word, Lord, and

2.   *last time*
let there be light.

2. Lord, I come to your awesome presence,
from the shadows into your radiance;
by the blood I may enter your brightness,
search me, try me,
consume all my darkness.
Shine on me, shine on me.

3. As we gaze on your kingly brightness,
so our faces display your likeness,
ever changing from glory to glory;
mirrored here
may our lives tell your story.
Shine on me, shine on me.

Words and Music: Graham Kendrick

50 Lord, unite all nations

2. Fill us with love, give us your peace,
   let grace abound and charity increase.
   From East to West may all be one in love:
   Lord, unite all nations in your love.

3. Teach us your love, teach us your peace,
   that joy may grow and happiness increase.
   Help us to work to make all nations one;
   Lord, unite all nations in your love.

Words and Music: Marie Lydia Pereira

51 Love is God's only law

1. Love is God's on - ly law for
God and hu - man - kind: love your God with
all your heart, your strength and soul and mind.
Love your neigh-bour as your - self, of ev - 'ry creed and
race, turn the wa - ter of end - less laws
in-to the wine of grace. Love is God's on - ly law,
love is God's on - ly law, love is God's wis - dom,
love is God's strength, love of such height, such
depth, such length, love is God's on - ly law.

2. Give to the poor a voice
   and help the blind to see,
   feed the hungry, heal the sick
   and set the captive free.
   All that God requires of you
   will then fall into place,
   turn the water of endless laws
   into the wine of grace.

3. Let love like fountains flow
   and justice like a stream,
   faith become reality
   and hope your constant theme.
   Then shall freedom, joy and peace
   with righteousness embrace,
   turn the water of endless laws
   into the wine of grace.

Words: Michael Forster
Music: Andrew Moore

52 Lovely in your littleness *(Jesus is our joy)*

Semplice, con gioa

1. Love-ly in your lit-tle-ness, long-ing for our low-li-ness,
long-ing for our low-li-ness, search-ing for our meek-ness: *D.C.*
Je-sus is our joy, Je-sus is our joy.

last time
Je-sus is our joy, Je-sus is our joy.

2. Peace within our pow'rlessness,
   hope within our helplessness,
   hope within our helplessness,
   love within our loneliness:

3. Held in Mary's tenderness,
   tiny hands are raised to bless,
   tiny hands are raised to bless,
   touching us with God's caress:

4. Joy, then, in God's graciousness,
   peace comes with gentleness,
   peace comes with gentleness,
   filling hearts with gladness:

Words: Pamela Hayes
Music: Margaret Rizza
© Copyright 1998 Kevin Mayhew Ltd.

53 Magnificat

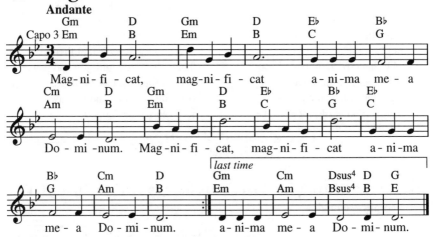

Mag-ni-fi-cat, mag-ni-fi-cat a-ni-ma me-a
Do-mi-num. Mag-ni-fi-cat, mag-ni-fi-cat a-ni-ma
me-a Do-mi-num. a-ni-ma me-a Do-mi-num.

Translation: My soul praises and magnifies the Lord.

Words: Luke 1: 46

Music: Margaret Rizza

© Copyright 1997 Kevin Mayhew Ltd.

54 May the Lord bless you *(A blessing)*

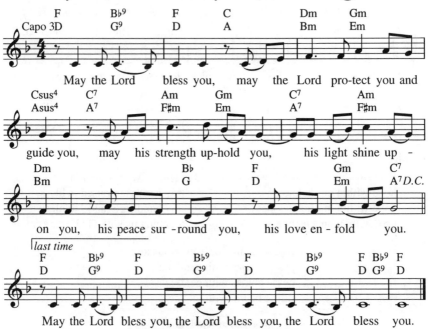

May the Lord bless you, may the Lord pro-tect you and
guide you, may his strength up-hold you, his light shine up -
on you, his peace sur-round you, his love en-fold you.
May the Lord bless you, the Lord bless you, the Lord bless you.

Words, based on a traditional prayer, and Music: Margaret Rizza

© Copyright 1998 Kevin Mayhew Ltd.

55 Meekness and majesty *(This is your God)*

Majestically

1. Meek-ness and ma-jes-ty, man-hood and de-i-ty, in per-fect har-mo-ny, the Man who is God. Lord of e - ter-ni-ty dwells in hu - ma-ni-ty, kneels in hu - mi-li-ty and wash-es our feet.

O what a my-ste-ry, meek-ness and ma-jes-ty. Bow down and wor-ship for this is your God, this is your God. God, this is your God.

2. Father's pure radiance,
   perfect in innocence,
   yet learns obedience
   to death on a cross.
   Suffering to give us life,
   conquering through sacrifice,
   and as they crucify
   prays: 'Father forgive.'

3. Wisdom unsearchable,
   God the invisible,
   love indestructible
   in frailty appears.
   Lord of infinity,
   stooping so tenderly,
   lifts our humanity
   to the heights of his throne.

Words and Music: Graham Kendrick

56 My first love (*Like a child*)

1. My first love is a blaz-ing fire, I feel his pow'r-ful love in me; for he has kin-dled a flame of pas-sion, and I will let it grow in me. And in the night I will sing your praise, my love. And in the morn-ing I'll seek your face, my love. And like a child I will dance in your pre-sence. O let the joy of hea-ven pour down on me. I still re-mem-ber the first day I met you, and I don't e-ver want to lose that fire, my first love.

2. My first love is a rushing river,
a waterfall that will never cease;
and in the torrent of tears and laughter,
I feel a healing power released.
And I will draw from
your well of life, my love.
And in your grace
I'll be satisfied, my love.

3. Restore the years of the church's slumber,
revive the fire that has grown so dim;
renew the love of those first encounters,
that we may come alive again.
And we will rise like
the dawn throughout the earth,
until the trumpet
announces your return.

Words and Music: Stuart Townend

57 My heart will sing to you *(Great love)*

1. My heart will sing to you be - cause of your great love,
a love so rich, so pure, a love be-yond com - pare;
the wil - der - ness, the bar - ren place, be-come a
bless-ing in the warmth of your em - brace. May my
heart sing your praise for e - ver, may my
voice lift your name, my God; may my soul know no o - ther
trea - sure than your love, than your love.

2. When earthly wisdom dims the light of knowing you,
   or if my search for understanding clouds your way,
   to you I fly, my hiding-place,
   where revelation is beholding face to face.

Words and Music: Robin Mark

© Copyright 1996 Daybreak Music Ltd, Silverdale Road,
Eastbourne, East Sussex, BN20 7AB, UK. Used by permission.

58 Now I know what love is

With a laid back jazz feel

Now I know what love is, now I know your Spi-rit is here, liv-ing deep with-in me, now I know love is real. 1. Death can ne-ver hide your love: your love lifts me high.

2. Darkness will not hide your love,
   shining like a star.

3. What could ever quench your love,
   love that changes hearts?

Words and Music: Mike Anderson

© Copyright 1999 Kevin Mayhew Ltd.

59 O give thanks

Medium fast, reggae style

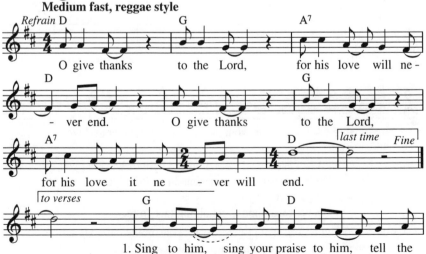

O give thanks to the Lord, for his love will ne-ver end. O give thanks to the Lord, for his love it ne-ver will end. 1. Sing to him, sing your praise to him, tell the

world of all he has done. Fill the na - tions with
ce - le-bra - tions to wel-come him as he comes.

2. Give him thanks for the fruitful earth,
for the sun, the seasons, the rain,
for the joys of his good creation,
the life and breath he sustains.

3. Let the heavens rejoice before him,
the earth and all it contains,
all creation in jubilation,
join in the shout, 'The Lord reigns.'

4. Let the hearts of all those who seek him
be happy now in his love,
let their faces look up and gaze
at his gracious smile from above.

60 O God, please listen
(In the shadow of your wings)

1. O God, please lis-ten to my cry, and give me an-swer.
I am a-fraid of what the fu - ture holds for me, O Lord.

Refrain

Let me hide, Lord, in the sha-dow of your wings.

Let me hide, Lord, in the sha-dow of your wings.

2. If only I had wings to fly
I would escape, Lord.
I'd fly as far as I could go
to find some peace of mind.

3. I feel defeated by life's
trials and disappointments.
My days and nights are spent in fear,
with no one I can trust.

4. But all of this I can survive
if you are with me:
my life is here, my life is now,
and I must carry on.

5. Within the shadow of your wings
I find my refuge.
You are the only one I have;
I count on you, O Lord.

Words, based on Psalm 54, and Music: Frances M. Kelly

61 O Lord, my heart is not proud

Calm

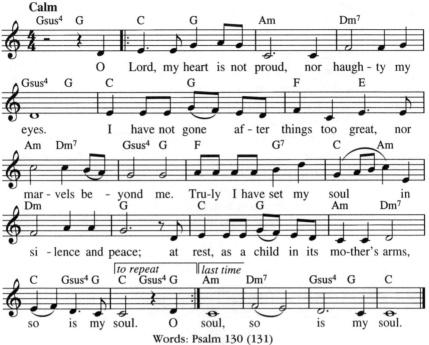

O Lord, my heart is not proud, nor haugh-ty my eyes. I have not gone af-ter things too great, nor mar-vels be-yond me. Tru-ly I have set my soul in si-lence and peace; at rest, as a child in its mo-ther's arms, so is my soul. O soul, so is my soul.

to repeat | *last time*

Words: Psalm 130 (131)

Music: Margaret Rizza

Text from *The Psalms: A new Translation,* translated by The Grail, England.
Used by permission of A.P. Watt Ltd, London.

62 One Father *(One God)*

Capo 3D *Refrain*

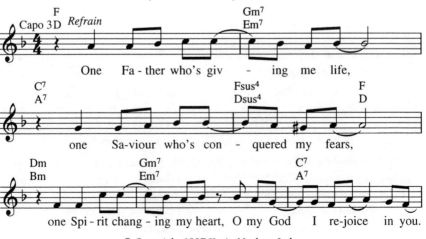

One Fa-ther who's giv - ing me life, one Sa-viour who's con - quered my fears, one Spi-rit chang-ing my heart, O my God I re-joice in you.

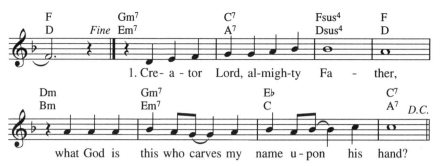

1. Cre- a - tor Lord, al-migh-ty Fa - ther, what God is this who carves my name u-pon his hand?

2. Lord Jesus, now enthroned in glory,
   what God is this
   who gives his life
   to set me free?

3. O living breath of God Almighty,
   what God is this
   who through my weakness
   sings his praise?

Words and Music: Gerard Markland

63 On this day of joy

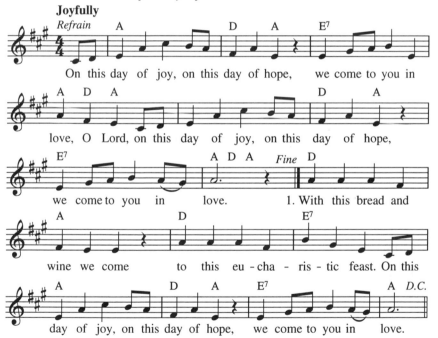

On this day of joy, on this day of hope, we come to you in love, O Lord, on this day of joy, on this day of hope, we come to you in love. 1. With this bread and wine we come to this eu-cha-ris-tic feast. On this day of joy, on this day of hope, we come to you in love.

2. Bread to be your body, Lord,
   wine to be your saving blood;
   on this day of joy, on this day of hope,
   we come to you in love.

Words and Music: Marie Lydia Pereira

64 Our Father

Words: Matthew 6: 9-13 and Luke 11:2-4
Music: Gerard Markland

65 Praise God in his holy place

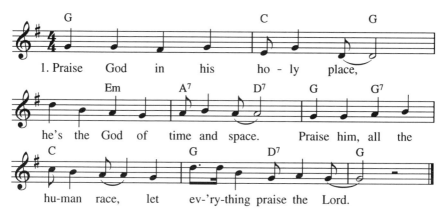

1. Praise God in his ho - ly place,
he's the God of time and space. Praise him, all the
hu-man race, let ev-'ry-thing praise the Lord.

2. Praise him with the ol' wood block,
   let it swing and let it rock,
   praising God around the clock,
   let ev'rything praise our God.

3. Praise him with the big bass drum,
   if you've got guitars, then strum.
   Now let's make those rafters hum,
   let ev'rything praise our God.

4. Praise him with the chime bars' chime,
   tell the bells it's party time,
   help those singers find a rhyme,
   let ev'rything praise our God.

5. Violin or xylophone,
   trumpets with their awesome tone;
   bowed or beaten, bashed or blown,
   let ev'rything praise our God.

6. Cymbals, triangles and things,
   if it crashes, howls or rings,
   ev'rybody shout and sing,
   let ev'rything praise our God.

Words: Michael Forster
Music: Christopher Tambling
© Copyright 1997 Kevin Mayhew Ltd.

66 Praise the Lord

Bouncy

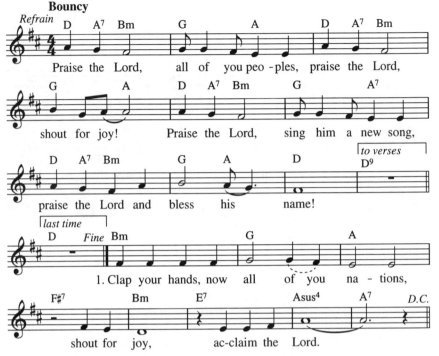

Praise the Lord, all of you peo -ples, praise the Lord, shout for joy! Praise the Lord, sing him a new song, praise the Lord and bless his name!

[to verses]

[last time] *Fine*

1. Clap your hands, now all of you na - tions, shout for joy, ac-claim the Lord. *D.C.*

2. He goes up to shouts which acclaim him; he goes up to trumpet blast.

3. Let the music sound for the Lord, now; let your chords resound in praise.

4. He is King of all the nations; honour him by singing psalms.

Words, based on Psalm 46, and Music: Mike Anderson

67 Rejoice, heavenly powers *(Exsultet)*

With an Easter feeling

Re - joice, hea-ven-ly pow - ers, sing, choirs of an - gels, ex - ult, all cre-a - tion, a - round God's throne.

Je - sus is ri - sen, sound the trum-pet of sal-va - tion.

Sing, dance and re-joice for Je - sus lives. *Fine*

1. Re-joice, O Mo-ther Church and sing, (Re-joice!)

(Re-joice!) bathed in the bright-ness of your

King! (Re-joice!) (Re-joice!) En-joy the

vic - to - ry he brings, (Re-joice!) (Re-joice!) re -

joice, re - joice, re - joice!

2. The price for Adam's sin is paid, (Rejoice! Rejoice!)
   by Jesus' blood we have been saved; (Rejoice! Rejoice!)
   he rose triumphant from the grave, (Rejoice! Rejoice!)
   rejoice, rejoice, rejoice!

3. This night will be as clear as day, (Rejoice! Rejoice!)
   the morning star is here to stay; (Rejoice! Rejoice!)
   and he has washed all guilt away, (Rejoice! Rejoice!)
   rejoice, rejoice, rejoice!

4. And now this Easter candle's light (Rejoice!, Rejoice!)
   dispels the darkness of the night; (Rejoice! Rejoice!)
   rejoice in justice, peace and right, (Rejoice! Rejoice!)
   rejoice, rejoice, rejoice!

Words, based on the Exsultet, and Music: Mike Anderson

68 Sanctum nomen

Tranquil

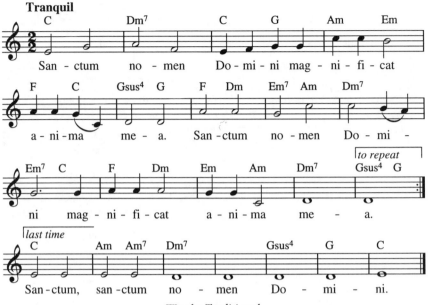

San - ctum no - men Do - mi - ni mag - ni - fi - cat
a - ni - ma me - a. San - ctum no - men Do - mi -
ni mag - ni - fi - cat a - ni - ma me - a.
San - ctum, san - ctum no - men Do - mi - ni.

Words: Traditional
Music: Margaret Rizza
© Copyright 1998 Kevin Mayhew Ltd.

69 See, he comes! *(Advent acclamations)*

Calmly

1. See, he comes! The Lord is near! And yet no one knows
when. See, he comes! The Lord is here! Let us all watch and pray.

Advent 2

2. See, he comes! The Lord is near!
   Our salvation's at hand!
   See, he comes! The Lord is here!
   Let us make straight his way.

Original text © Copyright Pierre-Marie Hoog S.J., L'Eglise St. Ignace,
75006 Paris, France. Used by permission.
English translation and music © Copyright 1999 Kevin Mayhew Ltd.

Advent 3

3. See, he comes! The Lord is near!
   He is here among us!
   See, he comes! The Lord is here!
   Let us sing and rejoice!

Advent 4

4. See, he comes! The Lord is near!
   Mary's 'Yes' gives him flesh!
   See, he comes! The Lord is here!
   Let us welcome the Word.

Originally written as Gospel acclamations for the Sundays of Advent of Year B, this can also be used simply as an Advent song.

Words: Pierre-Marie Hoog and Robert B. Kelly
Music: Jacques Berthier

70 Send down your Spirit

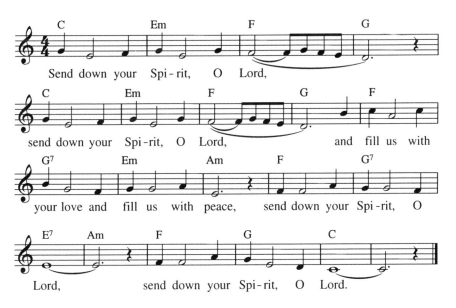

Words and Music: Mike Anderson
© Copyright 1999 Kevin Mayhew Ltd.

71 Send forth your Spirit, Lord

2. Lord, how great are your works,
   in wisdom you made them all;
   all the earth is full of your creatures,
   your hand always open to feed them.

3. May your wisdom endure,
   rejoice in your works, O Lord.
   I will sing for ever and ever,
   in praise of my God and my King.

Words: adapted from Psalm 103 (104) by Michael Forster

Music: Margaret Rizza

72 Share in the love of the Lord

Happily

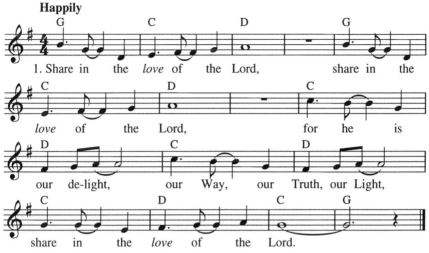

1. Share in the *love* of the Lord, share in the
love of the Lord, for he is
our de-light, our Way, our Truth, our Light,
share in the *love* of the Lord.

Change the words as appropriate: e.g. joy, hope, gifts, work, peace.

Words and Music: Mike Anderson
© Copyright 1999 Kevin Mayhew Ltd.

73 Silent, surrendered

Calm

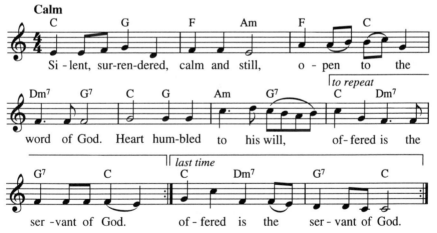

Si-lent, sur-ren-dered, calm and still, o-pen to the
word of God. Heart hum-bled to his will, of-fered is the
ser-vant of God. of-fered is the ser-vant of God.

For use at Pentecost

Come, Holy Spirit, bring us light,
teach us, heal us, give us life.
Come, Lord, O let our hearts
flow with love and all that is true.

Words: v1: Pamela Hayes, v2:Margaret Rizza
Music: Margaret Rizza

74 Sing, holy mother

Refrain

Sing, ho-ly mo-ther, bring-ing hope to birth, with the poor and hum-ble sing of hu-man worth. 1. Bles-sed are you a-mong wo-men, full of mys-te-ri-ous grace; hold-ing the hopes of cre-a-tion in your ma-ter-nal em-brace.

2. Stand with the lost and the lonely,
those whom the vain world denies,
join with the weak and the foolish,
humbling the strong and the wise!

3. Sing of the values of heaven,
shame our respectable pride!
Sing to the spurned and the fearful,
tell them no longer to hide!

Words: Michael Forster
Music: Kevin Mayhew

75 Sing it in the valleys

Brightly

Refrain

Sing it in the val - leys, shout it from the

moun-tain tops, Je-sus came to save us, and his sav-ing ne-ver stops. He is King of kings, and new life he brings, sing it in the val - leys, shout it from the moun-tain tops, Oh, shout it from the moun-tain tops.

1. Je - sus, you are by my side, you take all my fears. If I on - ly come to you, you will heal the pain of years.

2. You have not deserted me,
   though I go astray.
   Jesus, take me in your arms,
   help me walk with you today.

3. Jesus, you are living now,
   Jesus, I believe;
   Jesus, take me, heart and soul,
   yours alone I want to be.

Words and Music: Mike Anderson

76 Spirit of love

Gently

Refrain

Spi-rit of love, come fill us; Spi-rit of pow'r come, fill us; e - ven though we're young, we can still be strong in the Lord, in the Lord.

Fine

1. Do not let peo-ple dis - re - gard you just be-cause you are young. Show them by your love and faith you be - lieve in him.

D.C.

2. Give God thanks, he is our creator,
   he is Lord of all life.
   Brothers, sisters, we are one
   in his holy name.

3. Even when all around you seems
   to be just trouble and fear
   put your trust in Jesus Christ;
   he will guide you through.

4. Give yourself totally to Jesus,
   use your talents for him;
   people then will see your love
   and be drawn to him.

Words and Music: Mike Anderson
© Copyright 1999 Kevin Mayhew Ltd.

77 Take my hands, Lord
(Take my life)

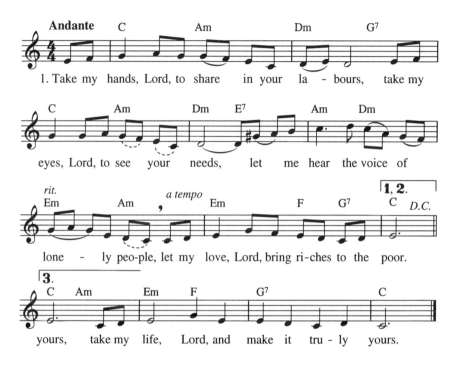

1. Take my hands, Lord, to share in your la - bours, take my eyes, Lord, to see your needs, let me hear the voice of lone - ly peo-ple, let my love, Lord, bring ri-ches to the poor. yours, take my life, Lord, and make it tru - ly yours.

2. Give me someone to feed when I'm hungry,
   when I'm thirsty give water for their thirst.
   When I stand in need of tenderness,
   give me someone to hold who longs for love.

3. Keep my heart ever open to others,
   may my time, Lord, be spent with those in need;
   may I tend to those who need your care.
   Take my life, Lord, and make it truly yours.

Words: Verses 1 and 3: Margaret Rizza; verse 2: Unknown
Music: Margaret Rizza
© Copyright 1998 Kevin Mayhew Ltd.

78 The kingdom of heaven *(The Beatitudes)*

The king-dom (The king-dom) of hea - ven, (of
new world (A new world) in Je - sus, (in

hea - ven) the king-dom of hea - ven is yours.
Je - sus) a new world in Je - sus is yours.

A yours.

1. Bles - sed are you in sor - row and grief, for you shall

all be con-soled; bles - sed are you, the gen - tle of

heart, you shall in - he - rit the earth. The

2. Blessed are you who hunger for right,
   for you shall be satisfied;
   blessed are you the merciful ones,
   for you shall be pardoned too.

3. Blessed are you whose hearts are pure,
   your eyes shall gaze on the Lord;
   blessed are you who strive after peace,
   the Lord will call you his own.

4. Blessed are you who suffer for right,
   the heav'nly kingdom is yours;
   blessed are you who suffer for me,
   for you shall reap your reward.

Words and Music: Mike Anderson

79 The Lord is my light

Larghetto

Words, based on Psalm 27, and Music: Margaret Rizza

80 There was one, there were two
(The Children's Band)

At a good pace

There was one, there were two, there were three friends of Je-sus, there were four, there were five, there were six friends of Je-sus, there were sev'n, there were eight, there were nine friends of Je-sus, ten friends of Je-sus in the band.

1. Bells are going to ring in praise of Je - sus, praise of Je - sus, praise of Je - sus, bells are going to ring in praise of Je - sus, prai - sing Je - sus the Lord.

2. Drums are going to boom in praise of Jesus,
   praise of Jesus, praise of Jesus,
   drums are going to boom in praise of Jesus,
   praising Jesus the Lord.

3. Tambourines will shake in praise of Jesus,
   praise of Jesus, praise of Jesus,
   tambourines will shake in praise of Jesus,
   praising Jesus the Lord.

Verses may be added ad lib, for example:

Clarinets will swing in praise of Jesus . . .　　Chime bars will be chimed . . .
Play recorders too . . .　　Glockenspiels will play . . .
Triangles will ting . . .　　Vibraphones will throb . . .
Fiddles will be scraped . . .　　Trombones slide about . . .
Let guitars be strummed . . .

Words: Christina Wilde
Music: Traditional American arr. Keith Stent

81 The table's set, Lord

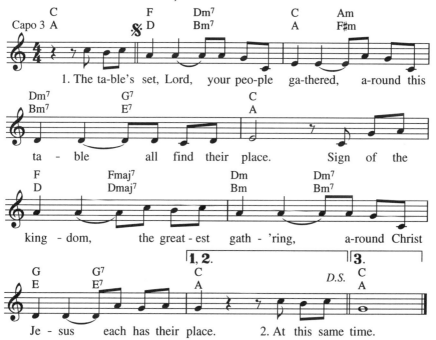

1. The ta-ble's set, Lord, your peo-ple ga-thered, a-round this
ta - ble all find their place. Sign of the
king - dom, the great-est gath - 'ring, a-round Christ
Je - sus each has their place. 2. At this same time.

2. At this same table in other places,
   so many people here in Christ's name.
   Those gone before us, who will succeed us,
   one single table throughout all time.

3. One Lord inviting, one church responding;
   one single bread and one cup of wine.
   May what we do here change and transform us,
   one single presence, Christ through all time.

Words and Music: Robert B. Kelly
© Copyright 1999 Kevin Mayhew Ltd.

82 To be in your presence

Very gently

1. To be in your pre - sence, to sit at your
feet, where your love sur - rounds me
and makes me com - plete. *Refrain* This is my de -
sire, O Lord, this is my de - sire, this is my de -

D.C. last time

sire, O Lord, this is my de - sire.

2. To rest in your presence,
   not rushing away,
   to cherish each moment,
   here I would stay.

Words and Music: Noel Richards

© Copyright 1991 Kingsway's Thankyou Music, P.O. Box 75, Eastbourne,
East Sussex, BN23 6NW, UK. Used by permission.

83 To your altar we bring

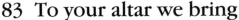

Refrain

To your al - tar we bring you these gifts of bread and
wine. Take, Lord, re - ceive, make them ho - ly and di -

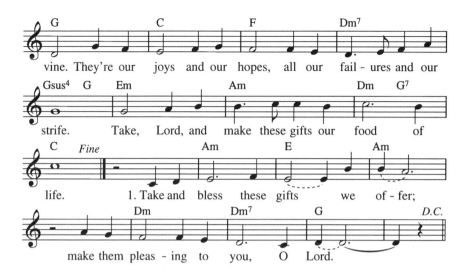

vine. They're our joys and our hopes, all our fail-ures and our strife. Take, Lord, and make these gifts our food of life.

Fine

1. Take and bless these gifts we of-fer; make them pleas-ing to you, O Lord.

D.C.

2. Take these gifts and make them holy by the pow'r of your Holy Spirit.

3. They'll become the body and blood of your Son, Jesus Christ, our Lord.

Words and Music: Julian Wiener

84 Veni, lumen cordium

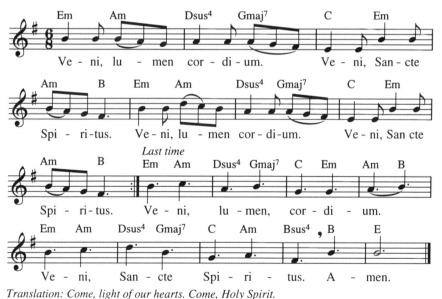

Ve - ni, lu - men cor - di - um. Ve - ni, San - cte Spi - ri - tus. Ve - ni, lu - men cor - di-um. Ve - ni, San cte Spi - ri - tus.

Last time

Ve - ni, lu - men, cor - di - um. Ve - ni, San - cte Spi - ri - tus. A - men.

Translation: Come, light of our hearts. Come, Holy Spirit.

Words ascribed to Stephen Langton (d.1228)
Music: Margaret Rizza

85 We are his children *(Go forth in his name)*

With life

1. We are his child-ren, the fruit of his suff-'ring,
saved and re-deemed by his blood; called to be ho-ly, a
light to the na-tions: clothed with his pow'r, filled with his
love.

Refrain

Go forth in his name, pro-
claim - ing, 'Je-sus reigns!' Now is the time for the
Church to a-rise and pro-claim him 'Je-sus, Sa-viour, Re-deem-er and

1, 2. *D.C. to vs. 2 & 3.* **3.**

Lord'.   Lord'.

2. Countless the souls that are stumbling in darkness;
   why do we sleep in the light?
   Jesus commands us to go make disciples,
   this is our cause, this is our fight,

3. Listen the wind of the Spirit is blowing,
   the end of the age is so near;
   pow'rs in the earth and the heavens are shaking,
   Jesus our Lord soon shall appear.

Words and Music: Graham Kendrick

86 We shall stay awake
(Advent acclamations)

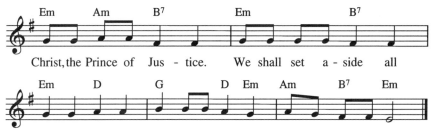

Advent 1

1. We shall stay a-wake and pray at all times, rea - dy to wel-come Christ, the Prince of Jus - tice. We shall set a - side all fears and wor - ries, rea - dy to wel-come Christ, the Prince of Peace.

Advent 2
> We shall set our sights on what is righteous,
> ready to welcome Christ, the Prince of Justice.
> We shall smooth the path, prepare the Lord's way
> ready to welcome Christ, the Prince of Peace.

Advent 3
> We shall plunge into the saving water,
> ready to welcome Christ, the Prince of Justice.
> We shall be reborn and rise to new life,
> ready to welcome Christ, the Prince of Peace.

Advent 4
> We shall hold with faith to what God promised,
> ready to welcome Christ, the Prince of Justice.
> We shall be attentive to his Spirit,
> ready to welcome Christ the Prince of Peace.

Originally written as Gospel acclamations for the Sundays of Advent of Year C,
this can also be used simply as an Advent song.

Words: Pierre-Marie Hoog and Robert B. Kelly
Music: Jacques Berthier

87 Wherever you go

Gently

Wher-e-ver you go I will go, wher-e-ver you live I will live; your peo-ple will be my peo-ple, your God will be my God. my God.

1. Christ and his Church are but one sin-gle bo-dy; Christ is the head, we fol-low where he leads.

2. Christ loves his Church and gave himself to save her;
   he made her holy, sinless, without fault.

3. Christ loves his Church, this is a sacred myst'ry;
   our human love is graced and speaks of God.

4. So may our love, like Christ's, be selfless giving;
   and in this giving, Christ is present here.

Words: Refrain based on Ruth 1:16, by Frances M. Kelly:
Verses 1-4, based on Ephesians 5:21-32, by Robert B. Kelly: Verses 5:8, Frances M. Kelly
Music: Frances M. Kelly

Other verses for weddings

1. We come today, in Christ a new creation,
   and in this giving we become as one.

2. Together now, our love can grow and strengthen;
   love is not selfish, we can share our joy.

3. And may our home become a place of welcome,
   an open door for all who pass our way.

4. We ask your blessing, Father, Son and Spirit,
   on all our friends and fam'ly gathered here.

88 Who can sound the depths of sorrow

With feeling

1. Who can sound the depths of sorrow in the Father heart of God for the children we've rejected, for the lives so deeply scarred? And each light that we've extinguished has brought darkness to our land: upon our nation, upon our nation have mercy, Lord. Lord.

2. We have scorned the truth you gave us,
we have bowed to other lords.
We have sacrificed the children
on the altar of our gods.
O let truth again shine on us,
let your holy fear descend:
upon our nation, upon our nation
have mercy, Lord.

3. Who can stand before your anger?
Who can face your piercing eyes?
For you love the weak and helpless,
and you hear the victims' cries.
Yes, you are a God of justice,
and your judgement surely comes:
upon our nation, upon our nation
have mercy, Lord.

4. Who will stand against the violence?
Who will comfort those who mourn?
In an age of cruel rejection,
who will build for love a home?
Come and shake us into action,
come and melt our hearts of stone:
upon your people, upon your people
have mercy, Lord.

5. Who can sound the depths of mercy
in the Father heart of God?
For there is a Man of sorrows
who for sinners shed his blood.
He can heal the wounds of nations,
he can wash the guilty clean:
because of Jesus, because of Jesus
have mercy, Lord.

Words and Music: Graham Kendrick

89 Who sees it all

1. Who sees it all, be-fore whose gaze is dark-est night bright as the day; watch-ing as in the se-cret place his like-ness forms up-on a face?

Refrain

God sees, God knows, God loves the bro-ken heart; and holds, and binds, and heals the bro-ken heart.

2. Who sees it all, the debt that's owed
of lives unlived, of love unknown?
Who weighs the loss of innocence,
or feels the pain of our offence?

3. Who knows the fears that drive a choice,
unburies pain and gives it voice?
And who can wash a memory,
or take the sting of death away?

4. Whose anger burns at what we've done,
then bears our sin as if his own?
Who will receive us as we are,
whose arms are wide and waiting now?

5. Whose broken heart upon a cross
won freedom, joy and peace for us?
Whose blood redeems, who ever lives
and all because of love forgives?

Words and Music: Graham Kendrick

90 Yahweh, I seek you

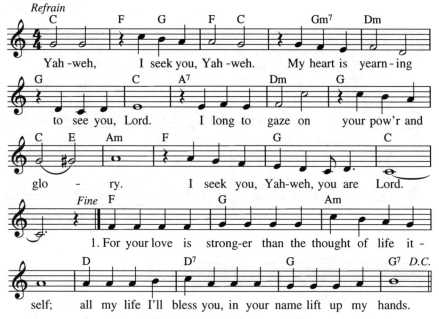

Refrain

Yah-weh, I seek you, Yah-weh. My heart is yearn-ing
to see you, Lord. I long to gaze on your pow'r and
glo - ry. I seek you, Yah-weh, you are Lord.

Fine

1. For your love is strong-er than the thought of life it-
self; all my life I'll bless you, in your name lift up my hands.

2. You have always been my help,
   on you I can depend;
   joyfully I sing now
   in the shadow of your wing.

Words, based on Psalm 63, and Music: Mike Anderson

91 You are beneath me

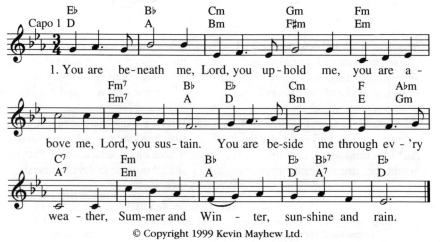

Capo 1

1. You are be-neath me, Lord, you up-hold me, you are a-
bove me, Lord, you sus-tain. You are be-side me through ev-'ry
wea - ther, Sum-mer and Win - ter, sun-shine and rain.

2. You go before me,
   you come behind me,
   you are my spirit,
   you are my guide.
   You are my star, Lord,
   leading me onwards,
   you my companion,
   here by my side.

3. You are my father,
   always sustaining,
   you are my saviour,
   you are my friend.
   You my beginning,
   you my true ending,
   yours be the glory,
   world without end.

Words: Graham Jeffery
Music: Kevin Mayhew

92 You are the centre

93 You are the light *(Enfold me in your love)*

2. You are the beauty that fills my soul,
   you, by your wound, make me whole.
   You paid the price to redeem me from death;
   yours is the love that sustains ev'ry breath.

3. You still the storms and the fear of night,
   you turn despair to delight.
   You feel the anguish, and share all my tears,
   you give the hope from the depth of my fears.

4. You are the word full of life and truth,
   you guide my feet since my youth;
   you are my refuge, my firm cornerstone,
   you I will worship and honour alone.

5. You have restored me and pardoned sin,
   you gave me strength from within.
   You called me forth, and my life you made new.
   Love is the binding that holds me to you.

6. You are the Way, you are Truth and life,
   you keep me safe in the strife.
   You give me love I cannot comprehend,
   you guide the way to a life without end.

Words and Music: Margaret Rizza
© Copyright 1998 Kevin Mayhew Ltd.

94 Your love's greater

2. Your ways are righteous,
   your laws are just,
   love is your promise,
   and in you I trust.

3. Your love is healing,
   your love endures;
   my life is changed, Lord,
   now I know I'm yours.

Words and Music: Mike Anderson

95 Gloria

2. Jesus, Saviour of all, Lord God, Lamb of God,
   you take away our sins, O Lord, have mercy on us all.

3. At the the Father's right hand, Lord receive our prayer,
   for you alone are the Holy One and you alone are Lord.

4. Glory, Father and Son, glory, Holy Spirit,
   to you we raise our hands up high, we glorify your name.

Words, based on the *Gloria* and Music: Mike Anderson

96 Glory to God, to God in the height
(Country Gardens Gloria)

1. Glo-ry to God, to God in the height, bring-ing peace to ev-'ry na - tion. Lord God al-migh-ty, Fa-ther and King, and the au-thor of sal - va - tion. 'Glo-ry!' let the peo-ple sing, let the whole cre-a - tion ring, tell-ing out re-demp-tion's sto - ry, as we wor-ship your name with thank-ful songs of praise for the love that is your glo - ry.

2. Jesus, the Father's one holy Son,
   all creation bows before you.
   You are the God, the God we acclaim,
   and we worship and adore you.
   Lamb of God, to you we pray,
   you who take our sin away,
   mercy, grace and truth revealing.
   At the right hand of God,
   receive our humble pray'r
   for forgiveness, hope and healing.

3. You, Jesus Christ, alone are the Lord,
   by your own eternal merit;
   sharing by right the glory of God
   in the presence of the Spirit.
   You alone are Lord Most High,
   you alone we glorify,
   reigning over all creation.
   To the Father, the Son,
   and Spirit, three in one,
   be eternal acclamation!

Words, based on the *Gloria* : Michael Forster
Music: traditional English melody, arr. Keith Stent
© Copyright 1995 Kevin Mayhew Ltd.

97 Sing glory to God *(Ash Grove Gloria)*

1. Sing glo - ry to God in the height of the hea - vens, sal -
   our King and our Sa - viour our God and our Fa - ther, we

va - tion and peace to his peo - ple on earth;
wor - ship and praise you and sing of your worth.

Refrain

Cre - a - tion u - nites in the pow'r of the Spi - rit, in

praise of the Fa - ther, through Je - sus, the Son. So

com - plex, so sim - ple, so clear, so mys - te - rious, our

God e - ver three, yet e - ter - nal - ly one.

2. Lord Jesus, the Christ, only Son of the Father,
   the Lamb who has carried our burden of shame,
   now seated on high in the glory of heaven,
   have mercy upon us who call on your name.

3. For you, only you, we acknowledge as holy,
   we name you alone as our Saviour and Lord;
   you only, O Christ, with the Spirit exalted,
   at one with the Father, for ever adored.

Words, based on the *Gloria* : Michael Forster
Music: Traditional Welsh melody, arr. Keith Stent

98 Holy, most holy, all holy the Lord
(Slane Sanctus)

1. Ho-ly, most ho-ly, all ho-ly the Lord, in
pow-er and wis-dom for e-ver a-dored. The
earth and the hea-vens are full of your love; our
joy-ful ho-san-nas re - e-cho a-bove.

2. Blessèd, most blessèd, all blessèd is he
whose life makes us whole and whose death sets us free:
who comes in the name of the Father of light,
let endless hosannas resound in the height.

Words, based on the *Sanctus*: Michael Forster
Music: Traditional Irish melody, arr. Keith Stent

99 O holy, most holy
(Ash Grove Sanctus)

O ho-ly, most ho-ly, the God of cre-a-tion, for e-ver ex-al-ted in pow'r and great might.
The earth and the hea-vens are full of your glo-ry. Ho-san-na, ho-san-na and praise in the height!

How bles-sed is he who is sent to re-deem us, who puts ev-'ry fear and in-jus-tice to flight; who comes in the name of the Lord as our Sa-viour. Ho-san-na, ho-san-na and praise in the height!

Words, based on the *Sanctus*: Michael Forster
Music: Traditional Welsh melody, arr. Keith Stent

100 O Lamb of God

1. O Lamb of God, come cleanse our hearts and take our sin a - way. O Lamb of God, your grace im -part, and let our guil - ty fear de - part, have mer - cy, Lord, we pray, have mer - cy, Lord, we pray.

2. O Lamb of God, our lives restore,
   our guilty souls release.
   Into our lives your Spirit pour
   and let us live for evermore
   in perfect heavn'ly peace,
   in perfect heavn'ly peace.

Words, based on the *Agnus Dei*: Michael Forster
Music: Hubert Parry, arr. Keith Stent

Index of Uses

THE EUCHARIST

PENITENTIAL RITE
Change my heart, O God — 15

GLORIA
Gloria — 95
Glory to God — 96
Sing glory to God — 97

INTERCESSIONS
Exaudi nos, Domine — 23

PREPARATION OF THE GIFTS
Blest are you, Lord — 13
Come on and celebrate — 19
On this day of joy — 63
To your altar we bring — 83

SANCTUS
Let our praise to you — 40
Holy, most holy, all holy
   the Lord — 98
O holy, most holy — 99

LORD'S PRAYER
Our Father — 64

SIGN OF PEACE
In the Lord is my joy — 37
May the Lord bless you — 54
Share in the love of the Lord — 72

AGNUS DEI
O Lamb of God — 100

COMMUNION
(see under COMMUNION below)

ADVENT
See, he comes — 69
We are his children — 85
We shall stay awake — 86

ASCENSION
Lift up your heads — 45
Praise the Lord — 66

BAPTISM
As the deer pants — 7
God cares for all creation — 29

CHRISTMASTIDE
Arise, Zion — 6
Lovely in your littleness — 52
Meekness and majesty — 55
Sing it in the valleys — 75

CHRIST THE KING
As the deer pants — 7
Come on and celebrate — 18
Father God, we worship you — 25
From the sun's rising — 27

Let the heavens declare — 41
Lift up your heads — 45
O give thanks — 59
Praise the Lord — 66
Rejoice, heavenly powers — 67
Sing it in the valleys — 75
We are his children — 85
We shall stay awake — 86

COMMUNION
Adoramus te — 1
Alleluia! Magnificat! — 2
As we are gathered — 8
Beauty for brokenness — 9
Come to me — 19
Father God, gentle Father God — 24
Give thanks with a grateful heart — 28
God cares for all creation — 29
God is love — 30
Healer of the sick — 31
Here is bread — 32
I look to the mountains — 35
I need you, Lord — 36
In the Lord is my joy — 37
Lord of life — 48
Lord, the light of your love — 49
My heart will sing to you — 57
Now I know what love is — 58
O Lord, my heart is not proud — 61
One Father — 62
Our Father — 64
See, he comes — 69
Send down your Spirit — 70
Share in the love of the Lord — 72
Sing it in the valleys — 75
The kingdom of heaven — 78
The Lord is my light — 79
The table's set, Lord — 81
To be in your presence — 82
Wherever you go — 87
Yahweh, I seek you — 90
You are beneath me — 91

CONFIRMATION
Come, Holy Spirit — 16
Dance in your Spirit — 20
Father God, we worship you — 25
God cares for all creation — 29
Send down your Spirit — 70

CORPUS CHRISTI
As we are gathered — 8
Jesus is risen — 38
Wherever you go — 87

CROSS
Let the heavens declare — 41

DEATH
All I once held dear — 4
Father God, gentle Father God — 24
God cares for all creation — 29
God is love — 30
How many years have I here — 33
The Lord is my light — 79

DISCIPLESHIP
Come to me — 19
From heaven you came — 26

EASTERTIDE
All heaven declares — 3
All I once held dear — 4
Dance in your Spirit — 20
Jesus is risen — 38
Rejoice, heavenly powers — 67

FORGIVENESS
Deep within my heart — 21
Gloria — 95
I look to the mountains — 35
I need you, Lord — 36
Listen to me, Yahweh — 46
Listen to my voice — 47
Lord of life — 48
Who sees it all — 89
You are the light that is
   ever bright — 93

FREEDOM
Dance in your Spirit — 20
Deep within my heart — 21

HEALING
Deep within my heart — 21
Healer of the sick — 31
I look to the mountains — 35
Let the heavens declare — 41
Listen to my voice — 47
My first love — 56
Silent, surrendered — 73
Who sees it all — 89
You are the centre — 92
Your love's greater — 94

HOPE
Love is God's only law — 51
On this day of joy — 63
Share in the love of the Lord — 72
Sing, holy mother — 74

HUMILITY
Sing, holy mother — 74

Index of Uses

JOY
Dance in your Spirit 20
In the Lord is my joy 37
Let us sing your glory 42
Lovely in your littleness 52
One Father 62
On this day of joy 63
Rejoice, heavenly powers 67
Share in the love of the Lord 72

LENT
Silent, surrendered 73
Who can sound the depths
of sorrow 88

LOVE
Come, O Lord, inspire us 17
Father God, gentle Father God 24
Let love be real 39
Let us sing your glory 42
Lord, the light of your love 49
Lord, unite all nations 50
Love is God's only law 51
May the Lord bless you 54
Meekness and majesty 55
My first love 56
My heart will sing to you 57
Now I know what love is 58
Share in the love of the Lord 72
Spirit of love 76
Take my hands, Lord 77
To be in your presence 82
Who sees it all 89
Yahweh, I seek you 90
You are the light that is
ever bright 93
Your love's greater 94

MARRIAGE
Wherever you go 87

MARY
Sing, holy mother 74

MISSION
From the sun's rising 27
We are his children 85

NIGHT
Lift up the light of your face 44

PEACE
Beauty for brokenness 9
Calm me, Lord 14
Come, O Lord, inspire us 17
Don't build your house 22
Father God, gentle Father God 24
Gloria 95
Here is bread 32
In the Lord is my joy 37

Listen to my voice 47
Lord, unite all nations 50
Lovely in your littleness 52
May the Lord bless you 54
Share in the love of the Lord 72
The kingdom of heaven 78
We shall stay awake 86
Who can sound the depths
of sorrow 88
You are the centre 92

PENITENCE
Change my heart, O God 15
Come to me 19
Listen to my voice 47
Lord of life 48
We are his children 85

PEOPLE OF GOD (CHURCH)
As we are gathered 8
My first love 56

POOR
Sing, holy mother 74
Take my hands, Lord 77

PRAISE, THANKS AND
WORSHIP
Adoramus te 1
Alleluia! Magnificat! 2
All heaven declares 3
All I once held dear 4
All through the years 5
As the deer pants 7
Be still, for the presence of
the Lord 10
Blessed be God 11
Bless the Lord 12
Come on and celebrate 18
Father God, we worship you 25
From heaven you came 26
From the sun's rising 27
Give thanks with a grateful heart 28
Gloria 95
Glory to God 96
Let our praise to you 40
Let the heavens declare 41
Let us sing your glory 42
Magnificat 53
Meekness and majesty 55
My first love 56
My heart will sing to you 57
O give thanks 59
Praise God in his holy place 65
Praise the Lord 66
Rejoice, heavenly powers 67
Sanctum nomen Domini 68
Send forth your Spirit 71
Sing glory to God 97
There was one, there were two 80

RENEWAL
Send forth your Spirit 71

SERVICE
From heaven you came 26
Take my hands, Lord 77

SILENCE
Be still, for the presence of
the Lord 10

SUFFERING
Beauty for brokenness 9
Let us turn to Jesus 43
Listen to me, Yahweh 46
The kingdom of heaven 78

TRINITY
Father God, we worship you 25
One Father 62

TRUST
Don't build your house 22
Father God, gentle Father God 24
I look to the mountains 35
Lift up the light of your faith 44
O God, please listen 60
O Lord, my heart is not proud 61
Spirit of love 76
The Lord is my light 79
There was one, there were two 91
You are the light that is
ever bright 93
Your love's greater 94

WHITSUN
Come, Holy Spirit 16
Come, O Lord, inspire us 17
Dance in your Spirit 20
Father God, we worship you 25
Send down your Spirit 70
Send forth your Spirit 71
Silent, surrendered 73
Spirit of love 76
Veni, lumen cordium 84
You are the centre 92

YOUTH
Spirit of love 76

Index of First Lines and Titles

This index gives the first line of each hymn. If a hymn is known by an alternative title, this is also given, but indented and in italics.

A

A blessing 54
Adoramus te, Domine Deus 1
Advent acclamations 69, 86
A healing song 47
Alleluia! Magnificat! 2
All heaven declares 3
All I once held dear 4
All through the years 5
Arise, Zion 6
Ash Grove Gloria 97
Ash Grove Sanctus 99
As the deer pants 7
As we are gathered 8

B

Beauty for brokenness 9
Be still, for the presence of
the Lord 10
Blessed be God 11
Bless the Lord 12
Blest are you, Lord 13

C

Calm me, Lord 14
Change my heart, O God 15
Come, Holy Spirit 16
Come, O Lord, inspire us 17
Come on and celebrate 18
Come to me 19
Country Gardens Gloria 96

D

Dance in your Spirit 20
Deep within my heart 21
Don't build your house 22

E

Enfold me in your love 93
Exaudi nos, Domine 23
Exsultet 67

F

Father God, gentle Father God 24
Father God, we worship you 25
From heaven you came 26
From the sun's rising 27

G

Give thanks with a grateful
heart 28
Gloria 95
Glory to God, to God in
the height 96

God cares for all creation 29
God is love 30
God of the poor 9
Go forth in his name 85
Great love 57

H

Healer of the sick 31
Here is bread 32
Holy, most holy, all holy
the Lord 98
How many years have I here? 33

I

I am the good shepherd 34
I look to the mountains 35
I need you, Lord 36
In the Lord is my joy 37
In the shadow of your wings 60

J

Jesus is our joy 52
Jesus is risen 38

K

Knowing you 4

L

Let love be real 39
Let our praise to you be
as incense 40
Let the heavens declare 41
Let us sing your glory 42
Let us turn to Jesus 43
Lift up the light of your face 44
Lift up your heads 45
Like a child 56
Listen to me, Yahweh 46
Listen to my voice 47
Lord of life 48
Lord, the light of your love 49
Lord, unite all nations 50
Love is God's only law 51
Lovely in your littleness 52

M

Magnificat 53
May the Lord bless you 54
Meekness and majesty 55
My first love 56
My going-home day 33
My heart will sing to you 57

N

Now I know what love is 58

O

O give thanks 59
O God, please listen 60
O holy, most holy 99

O Lamb of God 100
O Lord, my heart is not proud 61
One Father 62
One God 62
On this day of joy 63
Our Father 64

P

Praise God in his holy place 65
Praise the Lord 66

R

Rejoice, heavenly powers 67
Resurrection song 38

S

Sanctum nomen 68
See, he comes! 69
Send down your Spirit 70
Send forth your Spirit, Lord 71
Share in the love of the Lord 72
Shine, Jesus, shine 49
Silent, surrendered 73
Sing glory to God 97
Sing, holy mother 74
Sing it in the valleys 75
Slane Sanctus 98
Spirit of love 76

T

Take my hands, Lord 77
Take my life 77
The children's band 80
The kingdom of heaven 78
The Lord is my light 79
There was one, there were two 80
The Servant King 26
The table's set, Lord 81
This is your God 55
To be in your presence 82
To your altar we bring 83

V

Veni, lumen cordium 84

W

We are his children 85
We shall stay awake 86
Wherever you go 87
Who can sound the depths
of sorrow 88
Who sees it all 89

Y

Yahweh, I seek you 90
You are beneath me 91
You are the centre 92
You are the light 93
Your love's greater 94